Undiscovered NIAGARA

Rockway Falls.   - D. Free

- Linda Bramble

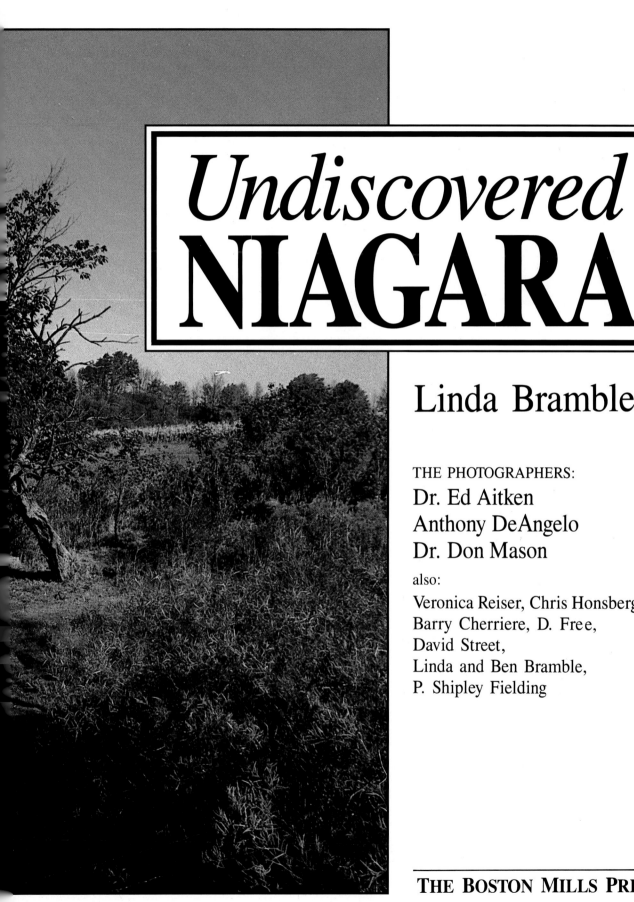

Undiscovered NIAGARA

Linda Bramble

THE PHOTOGRAPHERS:
Dr. Ed Aitken
Anthony DeAngelo
Dr. Don Mason

also:

Veronica Reiser, Chris Honsberger,
Barry Cherriere, D. Free,
David Street,
Linda and Ben Bramble,
P. Shipley Fielding

THE BOSTON MILLS PRESS

To my mother, Carolyn Falcone Palermo (1912-1988)
whose exuberant sense of discovery in the commonplace
was the inspiration for this book.

Canadian Cataloguing in Publication Data

Bramble, Linda
  Undiscovered Niagara

Bibliography: p.
ISBN 0-919783-61-9

1. Niagara Peninsula (Ont.) - Description and travel -
Guide-books. I. Title.

FC3095.N5A3 1989   917.13′38′044   C89-094236-6
F1059.N5B7 1989

Published by:
THE BOSTON MILLS PRESS
132 Main Street
Erin, Ontario
N0B 1T0
(519) 833-2407
Fax: (519) 833-2195

American Association
for State and Local History
Award of Merit

Winners of the
Heritage Canada
Communications Award

Typography by Lexigraf, Tottenham
Cover design by Gill Stead, Guelph
Printed by Khai Wah Litho PTE Limited, Singapore

The publisher wishes to acknowledge the financial assistance of The Canada
Council, the Ontario Arts Council and the Office of the Secretary of State.

Contents

6   Acknowledgements

7   Preface

9   Introduction

13   Chapter 1
       — *Grimsby*

25   Chapter 2
       — *Jordan and Vineland*

37   Chapter 3
       — *St. Catharines*

51   Chapter 4
       — *Pelham and the Short Hills*

65   Chapter 5
       — *Niagara-on-the-Lake and Niagara Falls*

82   Bibliography

83   Index

84   About the Author

Acknowledgements

Many people helped me present this book to you. I should like to thank Edith Brown and Florence Martin of Grimsby, Barbara Coffman of Vineland, Margaret Reed of Beamsville, Mary Lamb and Burt Murphy of Pelham, Arden Phair, Crystal Haeck and Robert Shipley of St. Catharines, John Field of Niagara-on-the-Lake and Glenn Meyers of the Niagara Conservation Authority.

When I needed them most, photographers Dr. Ed Aiken of Grimsby and Dr. Donald Mason of St. Catharines helped out by complementing our photographic collection with shots of their own. I thank them for their talent and their graciousness.

A special thanks to Robert Peabody of St. Catharines whose creative and knowledgeable eye directed me to many places in Niagara I had overlooked.

To Anthony DeAngelo, my son, I am grateful for his persistence, stamina and wonderful photographic contributions. His photographs of Niagara say it all.

And lastly, I am grateful to my husband Ben whose counsel, companionship and unwavering self-control (especially when I got us lost in the Short Hills) saw me through.

Preface

The Niagara region has internationally-known attractions which are centred in Niagara Falls and Niagara-on-the-Lake. In their push to reach these destinations, however, most visitors often miss some of Niagara's other fascinating features.

The intention of this book is to highlight some of those special places. At first, choice was a problem. What should I include? Then I realized that Niagara is so lovely, any errors I might make in choice are errors of ommission rather than of inclusion.

Undiscovered Niagara is for those of you who like to participate in a place by learning its history, feeling its pulse and exploring the places its own people enjoy. You're a special breed of traveller and it's my hope that this book will serve you well.

Introduction to Niagara

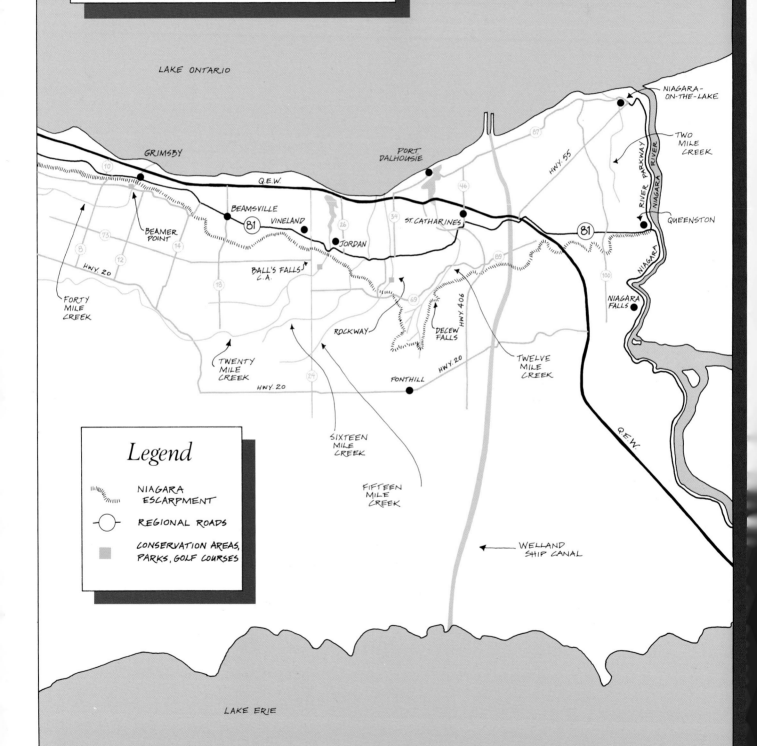

LAKE ONTARIO

NIAGARA-ON-THE-LAKE

GRIMSBY

PORT DALHOUSIE

HWY. 55

TWO MILE CREEK

Q.E.W.

BEAMSVILLE

VINELAND

JORDAN

St. CATHARINES

NIAGARA RIVER

RIVER PARKWAY

QUEENSTON

BEAMER POINT

HWY. 20

BALL'S FALLS C.A.

ROCKWAY

DECEW FALLS

HWY. 406

NIAGARA FALLS

FORTY MILE CREEK

TWENTY MILE CREEK

TWELVE MILE CREEK

HWY. 20

FONTHILL

HWY. 20

SIXTEEN MILE CREEK

FIFTEEN MILE CREEK

Q.E.W.

WELLAND SHIP CANAL

Legend

- NIAGARA ESCARPMENT
- REGIONAL ROADS
- CONSERVATION AREAS, PARKS, GOLF COURSES

LAKE ERIE

Introduction

Niagara Falls, with its wonder, justifiably attracts millions of people yearly. It is a pilgrimage every traveller should make. As beautiful and significant as the Falls are, however, there is much more to this region called Niagara than just the Falls. As a matter of fact, Niagara's falls are not the only ones of splendour.

NIAGARA'S TREASURES

For every major stream that empties into Lake Ontario, there are falls in other parts of the region that tumble impressively over the escarpment. What Ball's Falls, Swayze's Falls, Rockway Falls and DeCew Falls lack in water volume, they make up in ungarnished charm.

The region is a Canadian national treasure containing more than half of the 139 species of Canada's rare, threatened and endangered plants and animals. Nowhere in Canada, not even in British Columbia, can you find the rare species found here. Much of the area is Carolinian forest, named after the same vegetation zone found in North and South Carolina in the southern United States. It flourishes here because of our exceptionally mild climate in the shelter of Lakes Ontario, Erie & Huron. This is eastern Canada's "banana belt." It is actually part of a wider corridor of land that lies roughly south of Highway 401 from Toronto to Windsor.

At first glance the woods do not seem very different from other woods of the north where sugar maple, oak, beech and basswood are common. But a closer look reveals other kinds of trees, such as tulip, sassafras, red mulberry, Kentucky coffee and cucumber, whose normal range extends as far south as the Gulf of Mexico.

The mild climate of this zone also affects the wildlife. There are over 200 species of breeding birds here, about 40 percent of the breeding birds in Canada, birds such as the red-bellied woodpecker, yellow-breasted chat, the Acadian flycatcher and the tiny bluebird. Other birds, such as the mockingbird, usually associated with the South, find Niagara a perfect place to call home.

Although Niagara's Carolinian zone makes up less than a quarter of one percent of Canada's area, it is host to more rare species of plants and animals than any other region in the nation. The rarity and diversity of its ecosystem make it a remarkable forest.

What makes Niagara special is the fact that more remaining forest exists here than in any other area in the Carolinian zone. In the Windsor - London area, much of the forest has been cleared for farming. In Toronto and Hamilton, it has been cleared for urbanization. In Niagara, much still remains intact.

Excellent examples of the Carolinian forest and its magnificent community of plant and animal life can be found in the St. John's Conservation Area in Pelham (Chapter 4), The Glen in Niagara Falls (Chapter 5) and in the Jordan Valley (Chapter 2).

Most of Niagara is part of the flat and fertile Ontario plain. The countryside however, is broken by the north-facing cliffs of the Niagara Escarpment, "The Mountain" as we call it, has several abrupt gorges 93 - 109 metres (305 - 358 feet deep) that cut back deeply into the escarpment revealing different layers of sedimentary rock. It is one of the most complete highly fossiliferous and undisturbed geologic records of the Silurian Period in the western hemisphere.

Another prominent feature of the area is the eminence of Fonthill, which rises to a summit height of 260 metres (853 feet) above sea level, with its surrounding Short Hills. The Short Hills are composed of glacial debris which was deposited during the last ice age. Historic streams carved into these soft deposits, creating a picturesque region of steep valleys and hills which are reminiscent of the romantic hills of England's Dorset or the south of France.

VISITING NIAGARA

There are many ways to visit Undiscovered Niagara. You could bicycle to its 14 wineries along the wine route which is marked by purple road signs of grape clusters. (A map and guide entitled "Niagara Wine Region" is available at any Ontario Information Centre or by calling 1-800-268-3735/Toronto area 965-4008.)

Another lovely bicycle route has just been created along the Niagara River itself. You can locate the 2.5-metre-wide (8 feet) Niagara Recreation Trail anywhere along the Niagara River Parkway. It is ideal for joggers, walkers, bicyclists and people in wheelchairs.

Or you can drive. The Niagara River Parkway is perhaps one of the most scenic drives in Ontario. It follows the Niagara River on a peaceful 40-kilometre (25 miles) stretch from Fort Erie to Fort George in Niagara-on-the-Lake. It is also perfect picnic country, complemented by fresh fruit from any one of the numerous fruit stands that line the route.

Billed as the Gateway to Canada, it is a road that evokes Ontario's living history. For instance, when the river splits to encircle Grand Island, the American shore is less than a kilometre away. It was here that rumrunners and smugglers lined the shores to transport their illicit cargoes from Canada. At Navy Island, further downstream, the rebellious William Lyon Mackenzie declared a new Canada in 1837.

On the way to the Falls, the Parkway passes large farms, buildings and homes of architectural and historical significance, such as the colossal, 24-columned Italian Renaissance-style Toronto Power Company generating station, built in 1906 at the brink of the Falls. The driving force behind its construction was the eccentric Sir Henry Pellatt, who also built Casa Loma in Toronto.

After the Parkway leaves the Falls, the character of the countryside changes. Now it enters into the heart of the tender fruit country. Tidy orchards of peach, cherry, apple and plum are interspersed with rows upon rows of vinifera and hybrid grapes. Three of Canada's most distinguished wineries are on the route: Inniskillen, Reif and the newest, Willowbank. Inniskillen and Reif host tastings and tours. Inniskillen's wine loft is especially delightful for both the novice and connoisseur.

It is a romantic drive with dense woods climbing the banks of the river on one side. On the other, regal homes, both historic and contemporary, speak eloquently of more than a century of life in Niagara.

Another scenic drive is the west-east drive on Regional #81, or the "old No. 8 highway," as locals still insist on calling it. This route is ideal if you are approaching Niagara from the Ontario lakeshore. This is the old Grimsby - Queenston Road which ran through the centres of all the main villages that lined the lakeshore and which served as the major route between Niagara and Toronto long before the QEW was built.

It follows the well-defined shoreline of a former glacial lake, a sort of mini-escarpment, that was originally an old Indian trail. It has been a corduroy road and a stone road, once very busy with horses and buggies. All the stagecoach stops and hotels, many of which still exist today, had hitching posts in front of them with pumps and water troughs to water horses.

Today, it is a road of fruit stands, specialty shops and orchards, elegant old homes, historic churches, barns and farms, restaurants and watering holes.

It is the route of the old No. 8 highway that we are going to take as we journey through Undiscovered Niagara. There are many beautiful places in Niagara that go virtually unseen by visitors. This book is dedicated to revealing a few of those secrets.

Opposite:
Recreation Trail along the Niagara River Parkway. - Niagara Parks Commission

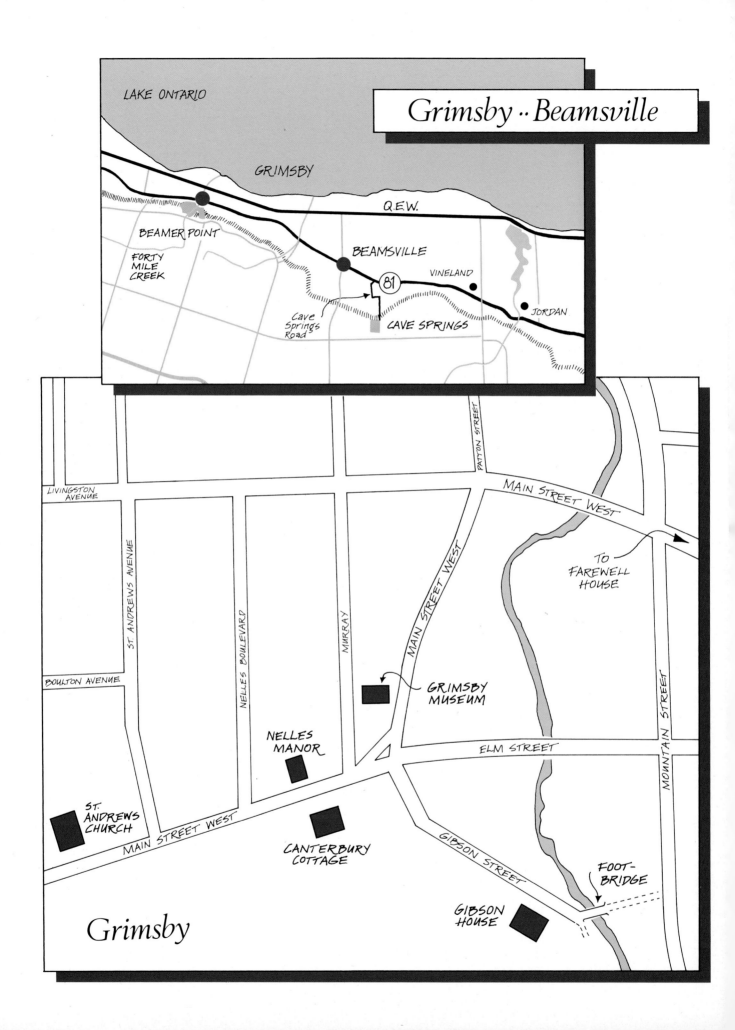

Grimsby ·· Beamsville

LAKE ONTARIO

GRIMSBY

Q.E.W.

BEAMER POINT

FORTY MILE CREEK

BEAMSVILLE

81

VINELAND

JORDAN

Cave Springs Road

CAVE SPRINGS

LIVINGSTON AVENUE

ST. ANDREWS AVENUE

NELLES BOULEVARD

MURRAY

PATTON STREET

MAIN STREET WEST

MAIN STREET WEST

TO FAREWELL HOUSE

MOUNTAIN STREET

BOULTON AVENUE

GRIMSBY MUSEUM

NELLES MANOR

ELM STREET

ST. ANDREWS CHURCH

MAIN STREET WEST

CANTERBURY COTTAGE

GIBSON STREET

FOOT-BRIDGE

GIBSON HOUSE

Grimsby

1
Grimsby

Grimsby is harboured on the rich plain where the Niagara Escarpment fringes Lake Ontario at its closest point. It is known as "the little town that fruit built," with beginnings as a thriving fruit growing, processing and shipping centre.

It was settled in the 1790s by United Empire Loyalists, who were the first to establish fruit farms in the area. Up until 1846 it was known as "The Forty," for its location on the Forty Mile Creek, 40 miles (64 kilometres) west from the Niagara River. The "Twenty, Sixteen and Twelve" Mile Creeks were similarly named for their relationship to the Niagara River.

Its older homes are an elegant testimony to the agricultural prosperity of Grimsby's early fruit farmers. There are many regal Regency, Georgian and Victorian estates that border the wide stretch of the old No. 8 highway as it runs through town. The interiors of some of these venerable residences can be seen during the Historical Society's annual "Harvest House Tour" in October. Throughout the year a self-guided "Historic Walking Tour of Grimsby" is available from the Historical Museum located on Murray Street. (The museum is one of the most advanced local museums in Niagara, housing its own exhibits as well as travelling exhibits from the Royal Ontario Museum.)

GRIMSBY'S PAST

The people and events that once sustained a community are the lifelines to its past. They explain why roads take certain turns, why fields lie fallow or are farmed. At the museum, Grimsby's fascinating early life has been imaginatively and artfully reconstructed. Among its displays are old photos of steamers full of tourists from Toronto, a penny farthing bicycle and a bloomer-style 1910 bathing suit.

The museum is the best place to start if you want to get a glimpse of this little town's fascinating past. Here you can see a model of the once magnificent round Methodist Campground Temple, modelled after the Mormon Tabernacle in Utah. The original temple was made from laminated oak planks, with a dome that rose 31 metres (102 feet) above the floor. There were no interior pillars or supports that would obstruct the view or break up the seating area.

It was here that over 7,000 worshippers met for ten days every summer to pray and enjoy the fellowship of other families like themselves. Known as the Chautauqua of Canada, it was also a significant educational and social event, since many of those attending came from isolated farms all over Ontario.

The Methodist Campground Temple, modelled after the Mormon Tabernacle in Utah, was made of laminated oak planks and rose to 31 metres (102 feet) above the floor with no interior pillars.
- Grimsby Historical Museum

Nelles Manor, Grimsby, built in 1788, is considered to be the oldest inhabited dwelling in Ontario. - Anthony DeAngelo

By the early 1900s the campgrounds had been sold to a private management company, which converted them into an amusement park that drew the largest crowds in Canada. On a summer's evening in the 1920s, Grimsby Beach was the place to be. There was a roller rink, a dance hall, a gas-lighted amusement park, and moonlight cruises on the lake with dancing on board.

A WALKING TOUR OF OLD GRIMSBY

It is always pleasing to discover the secrets of a lovely walk that is not primed for the tourist trade. Grimsby's is one such walk. A town's architecture is its functional sculpture and this delightful one-hour tour aptly illustrates the point by taking you past sophisticated estates such as the Georgian-style Nelles Manor and simple cottages such as the much smaller Canterbury Cottage.

The Nelles Manor on Main Street is considered to be the oldest inhabited dwelling in Ontario. (One older in Kingston recently burned down.) It was built in 1788. Canterbury Cottage, across the street, is in the Regency-style, built by Nelles's son, Charles, in 1852. Folklore has it that the catalpa tree in the front yard, with its twisted and ground-bent branches, was once used as an Indian marker. (The last Indians in the area that might have used it as a trail marker, however, probably predate the tree.)

St. Andrew's Church, down the block, is one of the oldest in Ontario. It was built of local stone by United Empire Loyalist settlers in 1818. It has a Wren-inspired tower with a rare Lych gate at the entrance walk. The handcarved wooden interior speaks to the artistry of another age.

Down Gibson Avenue, once known as the Mill Path because it led to the Nelles grist and saw mills, is one of the most enchanting little footbridges in Niagara. It crosses the rock-strewn Forty Mile Creek as it spills down the escarpment on its way to Lake Ontario. Nearby, a local resident has created a brilliant hillside garden along its banks with the original millstone from the Nelles mill centred in the midst of flowers, silently commemorating its past. This spot is the stuff of postcards and clichés, but the brook does babble and the flowers bloom and the salmon spawn in the spring. (Beamer Point is just above this spot, but more on that later.)

When Grimsby was settled, everything was around the creek, so the homes in this area are quite old. The Gibson home, at 14 Gibson Avenue, was the home of a Scottish stonecutter whose prosperous escarpment quarries provided the stone that built the Grand Trunk Railroad between Toronto and Sarnia, the St. Clair Tunnel, the Victorian Jubilee Bridge in Montreal and the Welland Canal.

Opposite: St. Andrew's Church built of local stone by United Empire Loyalists in 1818. It has a Wren-inspired tower with a rare Lych gate at the entrance. - H. Ed Aitken

Canterbury Cottage, built in 1852, and the catalpa tree in front once used as an Indian marker.
- Linda Bramble

*Gibson House, Grimsby, once the home of a Scottish stonecutter whose prosperous escarpment quarries
provided the stone that built the St. Clair Tunnel, the Welland Canal and the Victorian Jubilee Bridge
in Montreal.*
- Linda Bramble

The shopping district, busy, alive and very modern, belies Grimsby's nineteenth-century historical legacy. Prosperity is to "blame" for the alteration of its streetscape.

Grimsby never suffered the major economic decline that "historic" towns such as Niagara-on-the-Lake suffered. Benign neglect kept Niagara-on-the-Lake's shopping area intact. Grimsby, paradoxically, was too prosperous for its own historical good. Local businessmen could afford to build better structures than their nineteenth-century forebearers built, so the entire Victorian streetscape was replaced by one that was more contemporary.

The downtown's historical character and legacy was lost to progress with the lonely exception of one holdout in the heart of town, the gingerbread Farewell House. It is a fascinating anachronism that once belonged to the first pioneer doctor in the area, Dr. Woolverton, who had it built in 1839.

GRIMSBY'S EARLIEST RESIDENTS

Today Grimsby is growing rapidly as a dormitory town for Hamilton and Toronto professionals. Orchards have been replaced by subdivisions, and the town's population has doubled in size in the past few years. But Grimsby is no stranger to large communities of people.

Long before the first European "discovered" Niagara, there were upwards of 35,000 people living from Niagara-on-the-Lake to Grimsby — longtime residents of perhaps 2,000 years or more. They were the Neutral Indians, a settled, Iroquois-speaking tribe, whose cultural artifacts were found by most of the farmers in the region from its earliest days of settlement.

Flints, trail markers, mortars, pots, and remains of longhouses were brought to the surface as farmers cleared and tilled the land or as creek beds wore the shore away, revealing buried shards of cooking pots and drinking vessels. But the most spectacular finds have been the discoveries of Indian ossuaries or burial grounds.

Many of the sites had been disrespectfully looted and dismantled by curio hunters until October 1976, when a local builder unearthed an assortment of iron axes, copper kettles and beads. He thought he had found relics from an old pioneer homestead until he unearthed some bones and a human skull. At that point he carefully covered his find and called the Royal Ontario Museum. This began a contentious drama that lasted almost a year between the museum officials, who had explored the site further and realized it was indeed a prehistoric find of major proportions, and the Union of Ontario Indians.

The Farewell House, downtown Grimsby, once the home of Dr. Woolverton, the first pioneer doctor in the area, who had it built in 1839. - Linda Bramble

The Indians charged the curator on the dig, Mr. M.A. Kenyon, with "offering an indignity to human remains" in violation of the Cemeteries Act and placed an injunction on all activity. It was settled after a long, cold winter, during which the Indians agreed that the dig could continue as long as the bones were reburied.

When the dig was completed, Mr. Kenyon was able to fill in a major gap in the history of these ancient peoples. He and his crew found 374 skeletons from 58 different graves and deduced from the remains and their positions, condition and grave offerings, a rich history of a very sophisticated people. Among the artifacts they found were carved cedar spoons, cloth, beaver skins, pipes of limestone and clay, and a most interesting double-moulded vessel decorated along its sides. (Many of these artifacts are in the private collection at the Royal Ontario Museum in Toronto.)

The Neutrals, or Attiwandarons, were a hospitable, agricultural people, tall and tattooed, who took a neutral stance between the Senecas and the Hurons who were bitter enemies, permitting both warring Indian nations to pass unmolested through their neutral lands. The Neutrals

Indian dig on the original site before bones were re-interred by Dr. W. Kenyon, R.O.M. and his crew.

- Grimsby Historical Museum

were skilled artisans who supplied flints made of limestone from the outcrops of the escarpment. Their flint trade extended to Indian tribes all over northeast America. The discovery of conch shells from the Caribbean indicates they probably had trading connections with people along the Mississippi River, from the Gulf of Mexico to the Chesapeake Bay area. This trade gave them immunity from attack by their warring neighbours until 1650, when they were all killed or taken prisoner by the Seneca Indians following the Senccas' war with the Hurons. The white man could now provide these warring tribes with guns, so the Neutrals no longer had a trading edge. But the legacy of the Neutrals remains steadfast. It is the Neutral name Ongniaahra (spellings vary) from which Niagara is derived. (For more on the history of the Neutrals in Niagara, visit the Grimsby Museum. Publications by ROM Curator Kenyon, summarizing his amazing findings, are also available.)

THE HAWKS AT GRIMSBY POINT

From its earliest days, Grimsby has charmed the people who have come to know it. The wife of Upper Canada's first Lieutenant-Governor wrote "... I drank tea at Greens' and unwillingly left this fine scenery of which I had so slight a view . . . The Governor promises that I shall ride on the mountain above The Forty this season" (from Mrs. Simcoe's Diary, 1794). But people are not the only ones who find it a particularly joyful place to be. The birds (and those who watch them) agree as well.

Opposite: The Forty Mile Creek in Grimsby.

- H. Ed Aitken

"Kittling" Hawks at Beamer Point gracefully wheeling on circling updrafts. Part of the nearly 15,000 hawks who migrate north for the summer.   - Barry Cherriere

The farm at Cave Springs.   - H. Ed Aitken

Beamer Point, the highest point on the escarpment, is a bird-watcher's paradise. It lies on the flight path of Canada's most majestic family of birds, the hawks and their kin, as they effortlessly catch free rides on the invisible currents and thermals that rise between the escarpment and the lake.

In early spring, eagles, harriers, vultures, falcons and hawks can be seen gathering by the thousands, postponing as long as possible their long flight across the lake to their northern summer nests. There are several lookout points along the escarpment, but none equals the one at Beamer Point. (It is that high, protruding point you can spot from the QEW.) From here you can also get a hawk's-eye view of the patchwork landscape of the town of Grimsby below, plus an outline in relief of the intriguing geography of Burlington Beach, Oakville and Toronto.

In springtime these mighty birds give meaning to the word soar, gracefully wheeling or "kittling" on circling updrafts, then slowly descending in search of the next upward flow. They relax from their long journey north, many from as far away as Brazil and Central America. On a windy March day, when the temperature is about -7°C (20°F), you can expect to see the slotted dyhedryl wingtips of the imperial turkey vulture as he tilts his fingerlike wings to allow slipstreams of air to flow through, defying the sky to hold his weight. Or you might see the osprey, with bent, narrow wings, plunging out of the sky to catch a fish in the lake's still frigid waters, or get there in time to witness the long, pointed wings and tapered tails of the rocketlike peregrine falcons.

It is here you can also see the spectacular migration of thousands upon thousands of broad-winged hawks, with their black and white tails catching the sun. It is a serene sky ballet flown to the music of the wind — worth a springtime pilgrimage.

Beamer Point is reached by taking Mountain Road, following the Beamer Point signs up "the mountain" (as it is affectionately called) to the top. Turn right just before the Ukrainian Church. Park at the park entrance, a few metres down the road, and follow the footpath and then the white markers on trees, a ten-minute walk, to "The Point." It is on the far side of an old quarry where a gap in the greyish-brown escarpment shale provides a clearing for viewing. There is also a guardrail for safety. Take caution with children. Don't let them get ahead of you when you walk. The 93-metre (305 feet) slope is almost a sheer drop.

CAVE SPRINGS FARM

About 10 kilometres (6 miles) down the road from Grimsby on the old No. 8 highway (Regional Highway 81) is the community of Beamsville. Venture here in summer for a thrill of a different sort. On No. 8 highway, look for a road to "Cave Springs" on the right as you leave Beamsville. It's easy to miss, so be vigilant. Once you turn up this road, you tap into one of Niagara's richest veins of folklore and history.

There are stories that at Cave Springs Farm there is a lost cave holding the remnants of a civilization that flourished thousands of years ago, an underground lake, an aboriginal magnesium spring and a cave that provided refuge for escaping German spies during W.W.I.

But one of the most significant reasons Cave Springs Farm has been placed high on the list for preservation is because of the ice cave at the base of the escarpment. The site is reached by walking up an old lumber trail as it crosses the escarpment hill at its most gentle point. On top of the escarpment the white trail markers tell you you are also on the Bruce Trail. At a point where the escarpment separates slightly (called Adam's Steps), you shinny your way down to approach a most mysterious phenomenon of nature.

Before you see it, you will feel the icy draft of cold air upon your legs. You have found the ice cave. It is a haunting experience, particularly on a sweltering late-August afternoon.

Cave Springs Farm is not completely publicly owned. For that reason the Niagara Peninsula Conservation Authority (416-227-1013) must be contacted before you visit the site. It is not difficult to arrange an outing, but it is a courteous gesture to the present private owner of some of the property, Mrs. Margaret Reed. If you are lucky, she'll be your guide through this fascinating corner of Undiscovered Niagara.

Overleaf:
The Niagara Escarpment at Beamer Point overlooking Grimsby and Lake Ontario.   - Ben Bramble

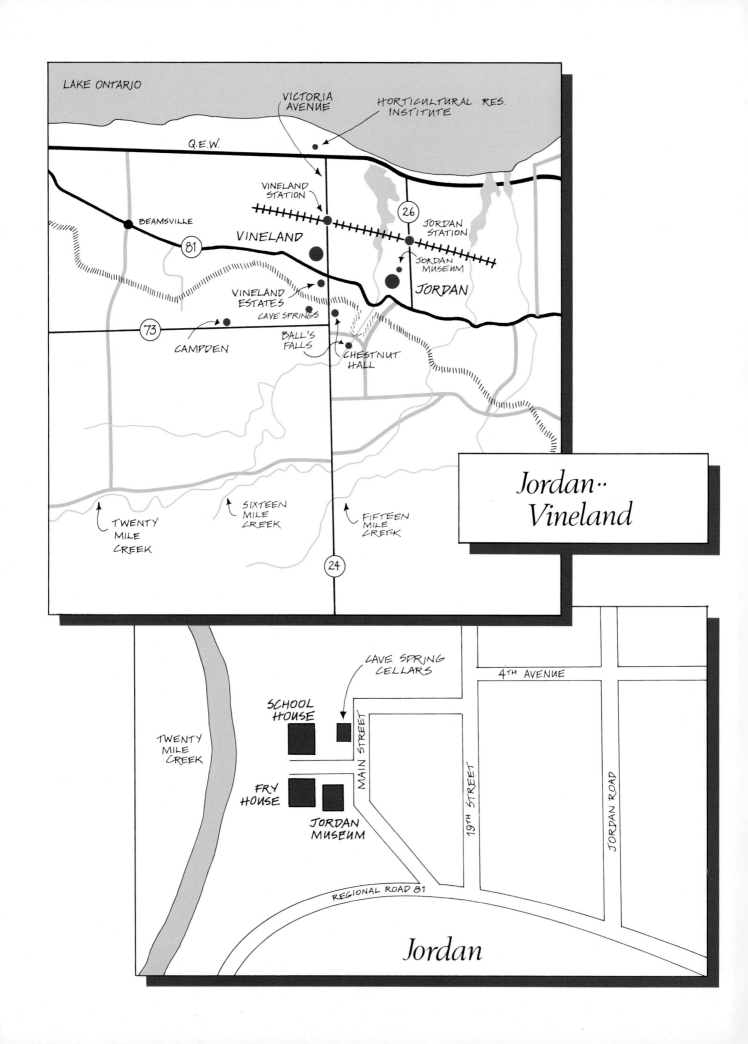

2
Jordan and Vineland

From Grimsby and Cave Springs Farm travel west along old No. 8 highway (Regional #81), Jordan and the Twenty are a country ride away. After winding and dipping your way through the undulating Jordan Valley, make a sharp left turn at the top of the road onto Main Street. Take this to the end and you'll be in the tiny one-street village of Jordan by the Twenty Mile Creek.

THE TWENTY MILE CREEK

The Twenty Mile Creek flows through some of the most varied landscape in Ontario — past spectacular waterfalls and the uplifted rocky dome of the Niagara Escarpment, through vineyards and orchards. Next to the Niagara River, the Twenty Mile Creek is the largest stream which crosses the escarpment in the Niagara Peninsula.

Around its banks early settlers built their homesteads. Towns were formed around trading, milling and transportation crossroads. The forces of man and nature worked together to decide which tiny clusters of homesteads would become the centres for future towns and cities. Other settlements disappeared, leaving only plaques and signposts to commemorate faded memories.

The area of the Twenty is an excellent example of the fickle manner in which certain centres live or die. Rockway Falls, for instance, was once a bustling salt springs. Today it is marked only by a community centre and a cemetery. Jordan Harbour, once a thriving port, is gone. Tintern, the birthplace of Governor General Roland Michener, is only a church and a sign. Mud Creek, a United Empire Loyalist settlement, has even fewer traces left. Glen Elgin, once a bustling milling community with promise as a prominent city centre, is now a pioneer relic village preserved at the Ball's Falls Conservation Area. (Located off Victoria Ave., Regional Rd. #24; exit QEW Victoria Ave. South.)

Yet other settlements of the Twenty prevailed. Campden, although no longer the leading village in the area, has survived. Vineland, traditionally an agricultural centre, and Vineland Station, built for fruit shipping with the Horticultural Institute established to aid farmers, carries on its farming legacy. And then there are the little jewels, Jordan and nearby Jordan Station.

EARLY SETTLERS

The first people to settle in the Jordan area were soldiers who had served with the illustrious Butler's Rangers and civilian United Empire Loyalists who were given land grants as a reward for their loyalty to the Crown.

In 1799 two Pennsylvania-German Mennonites arrived, scouting for a suitable place to bring the families they had left behind. They had also been loyal to the British Crown during the American Revolutionary War and now needed a place where they could worship free from the harassment of patriotic Americans.

They needed a place with farmland rich enough to enable them to live the simple style of life that marked their sect. The black walnut trees of Jordan were full and plentiful, a sure sign to Amos Albright and Abram Moyer that this was the best place to settle.

They bought 1,100 acres of land from the Loyalists living there and within months led 30 families back from Pennsylvania in horse-drawn covered wagons. They were thrifty and industrious people prepared to clear the wilderness by themselves and build a new life in Upper Canada. Although just as loyal to the Crown as the Loyalists, the Mennonites paid for the land they farmed.

So began Jordan, its early pioneers a strange and paradoxical mixture of political conviction and religious ardour, soldiers who bore arms and worshippers who were adamant in their refusal to do so. Yet their courage coalesced to forge prosperity out of the wilderness. That courage united them and the fertile Jordan Valley rewarded them.

Among the first group of Pennsylvania-German settlers to reach Jordan were the High brothers (originally spelled Hoch). Abraham High built a two-storey homestead from local clay mixed with straw and finished with clapboard. When it came time to turn over his home to his

Chestnut Hall, Vineland, the original home of Abraham High, one of the first Pennsylvania-German Mennonites to settle Jordan at the turn of the 18th century. - V. Reiser

eldest son, as was the Mennonite custom, the son built an addition to the side of the main house, an apartment for his father called a "doughty house." This addition is a distinctive feature of early Mennonite homes. High's house stands today, sturdy and solid, as Chestnut Hall, the home and antique shop of Mr. Barclay Holmes, on Victoria Avenue, on the escarpment above Vineland.

Abraham High sold part of his land to Jacob Fry who, in 1815, built a large two-storey log cabin of interlocking logs, covering it in a sheath of clapboard. In 1959 the home was moved to a site overlooking the spectacular 93-metre-deep (305 feet) Jordan Valley, where the first Mennonite Church had stood before a fire destroyed it, but more on that later.

The main street in Jordan began to take shape in 1837 when Jacob Snure purchased land from Abraham High, reasoning that the farmers of the Valley needed a village to provide goods and services. He surveyed the land and sold the lots to tanners, masons, tailors, innkeepers, merchants, blacksmiths, harness- and wagonmakers. They, in turn, built and lived in the Georgian and Victorian homes that still line the street.

Park the car and stop at Jordan's museum off the main street and pick up a copy of "A Walking Tour

Opposite: The old church at Ball's Falls Conservation Area. - D. Free

of Jordan." While you are there, note the particularly remarkable collection of fraktur art, dating back 200 years. (Fraktur is a form of Latin letter used in German printing.) Motifs such as hearts, tulips and birds colourfully decorate documents and manuscripts: a lost art.

Two other buildings are part of the museum complex. One is an old schoolhouse built in 1859 that houses one of the most unusual pioneer collections of farm implements in Ontario, including a rare giant fruit press.

THE FRY HOUSE

The second building is the two-storey log cabin that Jacob Fry built and where his son, Samuel Fry, eventually lived. Samuel Fry became "a weaver of unusual merit, of great importance to the history of Canada's textile heritage." His furniture, looms, textiles, patterns and account books have been preserved there.

The Fry House is the only example of a home of a pioneer farmer-craftsman in Ontario furnished with original materials. It is thoughtfully designed, featuring built-in cupboards, draw curtains, swinging lamps and a kitchen equipped with copper-lined kettles and a large, comforting open hearth. Plain and fancy coverlets handwoven by this master craftsman are now heirlooms in use today in many Ontario homes.

In a quirk of fate, Abraham High died in 1856 and was buried in the church cemetery where The Fry House,

The Fry House, Jordan, built in 1815, is the only example in Ontario of a home of a pioneer-craftsmen (weaver) furnished with original materials.
- D. Free

The mysterious grave of Nancy High at the cemetery beside the Fry House, Jordan. - V. Reiser

moved from its original location on High's property, now stands. The two old neighbours meet again!

The church cemetery beside the Fry House has few graves, but the ones it does cloister hold a mystery no one has yet solved. Buried beneath a grove of sturdy black walnut trees lies Abraham High, his wife, and daughter-in-law, Nancy. Beside the tilting upright stones of her friends and neighbours are stones resting on the ground.

In the centre is Abraham High, Sr., who died at a venerable 90. On his right lies his wife, Margaret, who died at a hearty 81. On his left is a stone headed by a weeping willow and inscribed "Nancy, wife of Abraham High, Jr., died April 18, 1856, aged 33 years, 10 months and 23 days." The exact span of one's life in those days was an apparently significant detail.

So far, no mystery. But as you walk to the right, reading the inscriptions, you will be struck by a second gravestone, marked by a hand with a forefinger pointing up, which reads, "Nancy, wife of Abraham High, died April 18, 1856, died age 33 years."

Under which grave does Nancy High lie? What accounts for this breach of burial?

EARLY LIFE REVISITED

Because Jordan and most of the idyllic spots along the Twenty remain unspoiled, they offer a rare opportunity to think about the links we have with the people who first settled there. Only time disconnects us from them, except in early spring and late fall.

From the last week of February through the middle of March, the sap of the Vineland Quarries Sugar Bush is running. It is a great opportunity to tramp through the woods and see firsthand how the pioneers and Indians collected this sweet delicacy. The Niagara Peninsula Conservation Authority operates the Sugar Bush and taps nearly 200 trees annually, demonstrating methods of syrup-making from ancient to modern times. Maple products are for sale in the sugar shanty. (The Sugar Bush is located off Cherry Avenue and 5th Concession in Vineland. Contact the Niagara Peninsula Conservation Authority at (416) 227-1013 for more information.)

The fall is probably the best time to visit Jordan, particularly on the first Saturday after Thanksgiving. This is when the village springs to life — pioneer life that is.

Pioneer Day in Jordan. - Don Mason

The sugar bush at Vineland Quarries.
- Niagara Peninsula Conservation Authority

Overleaf: The cemetery at Rockway, once a thriving community.
- Linda Bramble

The ladies dress in calico and lace, and the men either become part of the regiment of soldiers on parade, firing their muskets in practice over the Jordan Valley, or they became tinsmiths, blacksmiths and apple-pressers.

These are Pioneer Days, when the crisp autumn air is filled with the aroma of hot apple cider and freshly baked apple goodies. They even get the old fruit press working to help animate a century-old way of life.

Along Jordan's interesting little main street are antique dealers and craftsmen. But be sure not to miss a chance to stop into one of Ontario's most promising new wineries, Cave Spring Cellars. Already they have won top awards for their chardonays and rieslings. Len Pennachetti, president, attributes it to the fact his vineyards are located on the Niagara bench, the sloping land at the foot of the Niagara escarpment. He theorizes that the bench is viticulturally different from the low-lying Lake Ontario plain below. The sloping vineyards allow better drainage and the heavy clay soils of the bench tend to produce less foilage and more fruit than the lighter, sandier soils of the plain. The wine bar at Cave Spring Cellars offers an opportunity to sample his latest vintages.

THE HORTICULTURAL RESEARCH INSTITUTE OF ONTARIO

If you are a gardener or a farmer at heart, or simply want to find an out-of-the-way hideaway of magnificent parkland on a small scale, you won't want to miss the Horticultural Institute of Ontario at Vineland Station. (Reach it by exiting the QEW at Victoria Avenue North, or take Victoria Avenue from Regional Road 81.)

Inside the Administrative Building there are publications available (most are free) with advice on everything from "How to buy a silo" to "How to bake bread." Although there is little to see at the experimental station itself, the grounds and rhododendron garden are splendidly cool and private places in mid-summer. There are all sorts of distinctive ornamental trees and shrubs discreetly labelled for the interested.

This woodlot is secreted away on the other side of the road and is reached by an underground pedestrian tunnel. Find the tunnel by parking in the small parking lot to the left as you enter the Horticultural Institute from Victoria Avenue. From this lot you can see the footpath leading to the tunnel. It's a delightful walk, full of horticultural surprises.

The Horticultural Research Institute of Ontario was established in 1906 to benefit the region's farmers. It experiments with grapes, for instance, and has had a significant impact on North American grape production. All deChaunac, Seibel and Chelois grapes originated at this experimental research station.

Fruit varieties are also tested, along with experiments on processing and storing methods. They are still looking for improved grapes, particularly the white varieties. They seek a yield of European-type fruit with high sugar and low acid content, one that is winter hardy, disease resistant, and requires no thinning. "Vivant" is their most recent release that seems to fulfill these criteria.

VINELAND ESTATES WINERY

There is another delightful surprise in store for wine lovers just down the road at Vineland Estates Winery. Take Victoria Avenue south from the QEW exit towards Vineland, cross old No. 8 highway (Regional #81), and go up the "mountain" to Moyer Road and turn right. About half a mile down the road is the gently rolling vineyard of St. Urban, one of the farms for Vineland Estates Winery.

Vineland Estates is one of the few wineries in Niagara that uses only the vinifera and hybrid grapes it grows on its own carefully watched farms to produce its Germanic-style wines. Their new house wine is made from the classic vinifera and hybrid grapes, with not even the vapours from the old foxy labruscas affecting this lovely and affordable table wine.

Back onto old No. 8 highway (Regional #81), travel east to the Garden City, St. Catharines.

Opposite:
The vineyards at Vineland Estate Winery. - David Street

Rockway Gorge.   - Linda Bramble

Harvest time.   - Don Mason

Opposite:
Below the Upper Falls in Jordan.   - D. Free

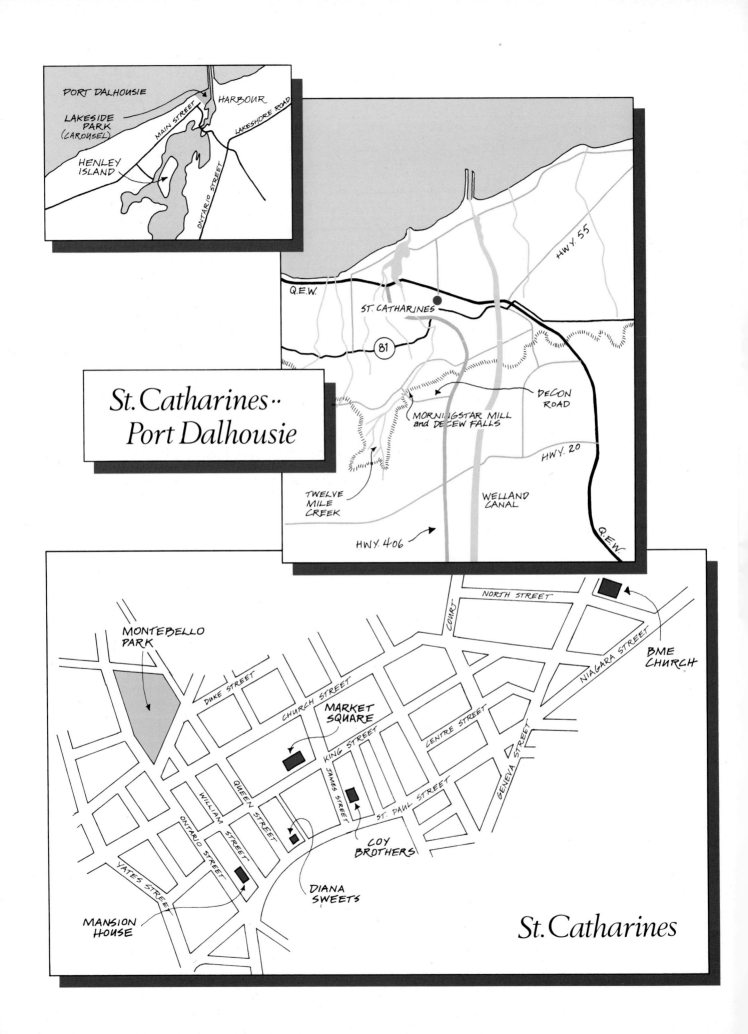

St. Catharines··
Port Dalhousie

PORT DALHOUSIE
LAKESIDE PARK (CAROUSEL)
HARBOUR
MAIN STREET
LAKESHORE ROAD
ONTARIO STREET
HENLEY ISLAND

Q.E.W.
HWY. 55
ST. CATHARINES
81
DeCON ROAD
MORNINGSTAR MILL and DECEW FALLS
HWY. 20
TWELVE MILE CREEK
WELLAND CANAL
HWY. 406
Q.E.W.

MONTEBELLO PARK
NORTH STREET
COURT
NIAGARA STREET
BME CHURCH
DUKE STREET
CHURCH STREET
MARKET SQUARE
KING STREET
CENTRE STREET
JAMES STREET
ST. PAUL STREET
GENEVA STREET
WILLIAM STREET
QUEEN STREET
ONTARIO STREET
COY BROTHERS
YATES STREET
DIANA SWEETS
MANSION HOUSE

St. Catharines

3
St. Catharines

St. Catharines routinely takes visitors by surprise. It is a comfortable and undemanding early Ontario town set in the middle of the rich and fertile Ontario plain.

It prospered as a port in the days when the old Welland Canal wended its way directly behind the shops and businesses of its main street, St. Paul. The secrets of those early canal days still echo in the same shops in whose original buildings sailors, merchants, ships' chandlers and traders transacted their business.

Five generations have carried on the Coy Brothers business, for instance. In 1850 it was a "Shelf and Heavy Hardware" store, today its James Street shelves hold everything from hinges, appliances, knives and baskets to crystal, china, candles, cards and toys.

Of another era, but no less distinctive, is Diana Sweets on St. Paul Street, a *real* old-fashioned soda fountain with a marble-top lunch counter, gumwood booths, and the best sodas and sundaes in town. Here you find none of the "instant-old" decor that is found so often in towns that cater to the tourist trade.

The Mansion House, another unspoiled original, is still a watering hole much loved by the locals. It has been a pub since the early days of the canal. William Hamilton Merritt built it as a hotel and coach stop in 1816 and conducted business from an office in one of the rooms at the back.

Country life merged with commerce at the Market Square. Today farmers and vendors still set up their stalls, as they have for over 100 years, every Tuesday, Thursday and Saturday. Under the yellow canopy, they sell farm-fresh produce, fresh poultry, magnificent locally made cheeses, fish, and flowers grown from local greenhouses. (Niagara's growers are the number-one producers of flowers in Canada.)

When the water level in the creek which powered Merritt's flour and saw mills dropped dangerously low in dry months, he proceeded with plans to build a canal — the Welland Canal. The rest is the history of a world-renowned inland waterway that eventually connected the land-locked American midwest to the Atlantic Ocean.

Nowhere else in the world are large ocean-going vessels lifted as high, 75 metres (246 feet) over a distance of 44 kilometres (27 miles). Now a part of the St. Lawrence Seaway System, it has played a significant role in the growth of both the United States and Canada. Even though it is a major tourist attraction and not truly "undiscovered," don't miss the wonder of watching a huge ship "climb the mountain." From Lock No. 3 viewing platform you can watch ocean-going vessels as they are lifted up over the escarpment through the intricate and massive system of locks. The St. Catharines museum nearby has a remarkable working model of the locks that helps to explain visually the principles behind this mammoth technology.

William Hamilton Merritt, St. Catharines, the man who built the Welland Canal.
- Don Mason

The middle of the nineteenth century provided the setting for one of the most dramatic human encounters in the nation's history. In the 1840s St. Catharines was fast becoming a world-class health spa. Mineral and salt waters had been discovered beneath the waters of the Twelve Mile Creek. By 1850 artesian wells pumped hundreds of gallons of water a day to nearby resort hotels that catered to bathers from all over the continent. They were seeking a hydropathic cure for everything from

Overleaf: A ship docked on the Welland Canal. - Don Mason

rheumatism to migraine. The temperate climate and medicinal waters enticed many wealthy southern plantation owners and their families to spend the entire summer season here, giving the town a decidedly southern air.

When the Civil War broke out, many distinguished southerners moved here for the duration of the conflict, some to rest and get away from the turmoil and strife, and others to become more fiercely embroiled in it. It was in a stately home on Park Street that the Confederate Secret Service set up one of its headquarters and planned numerous attacks on the Union from flanking points in the North. Just after the war ended, implicating papers were found there addressed to John Wilkes Booth!

Escaped Confederate soldiers and Union army draft-dodgers made a volatile mix of men and politics in the town's taverns. To add to the fire, St. Catharines was also the haven for hundreds of fugitive slaves who sought freedom on Canadian soil. Their church, the British Methodist Episcopal (BME), built in 1855, still stands on Geneva Street, with an active congregation — a tribute to their endurance and courage.

What did these men and women say to one another when North met South, master met slave? What fires of indignation burned? What peace did they make?

Scenes of such encounters can become even more vivid when contemplated from a park bench in the city's oldest park, Montebello. Bands still play in the turn-of-the-century band shell and pancake breakfasts are still held in the century-old pavilion.

The neighbourhoods surrounding the park, especially on Queen and Yates streets, are extraordinary examples of early Ontario architecture (Italianate, neo-Gothic, neo-Tudor, Georgian, etc.) and well worth a leisurely walk.

St. Catharines was settled in the late 1700s by Americans from New York state who preferred to remain loyal to the Crown. Besides being rich in farmland and water power, the area was far enough from the American border — 48 kilometres (30 miles) from Buffalo — but close enough to frontier markets.

The Welland Hotel, St. Catharines, when it was a lavish spa attracting thousands of visitors a year to its mineral baths. — St. Catharines Historical Museum

The old Welland Canal along the Merritt Trail in St. Catharines. Note Brock University in the distance.

- Don Mason

Montebello Park, St. Catharines, designed a century ago by Olmstead, the same man who designed Central Park in New York City. The pavilion and bandstand date back to the turn of the century.

- Anthony DeAngelo

The marketsquare and Court House in St. Catharines. — Anthony DeAngelo

The marketsquare a century ago. — St. Catharines Historical Museum

MORNINGSTAR MILL AND DECEW FALLS

Creeks and streams flowing over the escarpment also provided a plentiful source of water power, thereby encouraging the growth of numerous grist, saw, and textile mills.

At DeCew Falls, just on the outskirts of the city centre, one mill remains intact, Morningstar Mill, built in 1872. It was originally known as Mountain Mill until Wilson Morningstar purchased it in 1883. For the next 50 years he ground grain into flour, keeping one-twelfth as payment.

The mill, standing beside Beaver Dam's Creek, was one of the most advanced mills of its kind, fitted with a water turbine rather than a water wheel. Although the mill stopped grinding in 1933, the original works are still operative; the millstone, hopper, hoist and grinders sit poised, just waiting for someone to crank them up again. Visitors are welcome to step inside for a guided tour of the mill's cranks and gears, and a lesson on how they operated. You can almost hear the clatter of the sifter and smell the fresh-ground grain.

There is a lovely foliage-framed view of the DeCew Falls found by walking along the Bruce Trail just behind the mill. The fence along the trail has been broken in many places and the ground falls away rather quickly, so caution is advised, particularly with children. The view of the narrow valley and its great cliffs and boulders has been a secret destination for travellers for many, many years.

Morningstar Mill (1872) at DeCew Falls, St. Catharines.   - Anthony DeAngelo

PORT DALHOUSIE

Just north of the city centre is the old port of Port Dalhousie. Although its mailing address is St. Catharines, its history as a town is quite distinctive.

Three of the four successive Welland Canals travelled through the town centre. Visible reminders of these canals overlap in the harbour today. You can see parts of the old floating towpath in Martindale Pond, locks from the second and third canals, and the old customs house.

At the turn of the century, Port Dalhousie moored so many ships in her yards it is said a person could walk the entire width of the canal by jumping from deck to deck amidst a "sea of masts." Passers-by were so close to schooners and steamers they could almost shake hands with the sailors on deck.

By the 1900s Lakeside Park, on Port Dalhousie's beach, had become a mecca for bathers and picnickers. Its midway and carousel attracted thousands of visitors from Toronto and Buffalo. The kewpie dolls are gone, but the carousel remains, still taking its travellers on musical journeys, on the original intricately carved lions, tigers and horses, to places in the heart — still, and in perpetuity, for only a nickle a ride!

The marina, the walk on the pier to the outer lighthouse, the restaurants and boutiques are all delightful ways to spend an afternoon, but a visit to nearby Henley Island will give you a view of Port Dalhousie most tourists miss.

This is the home of the Royal Canadian Henley Regatta, established in 1880. With the exception of two years during World War I, it has run continuously ever since. It has full international facilities, a 2,000-metre (2,187 yards) course and a covered grandstand that seats 3,000 spectators.

Several regattas are held here during the season, but the best known, the Henley Regatta (held the first week in August), is now the largest in the world. The island is untouched by commerce, so even if there are no races, it still provides a lovely afternoon's walk. Unless there is ice on the pond, you are sure to find rowers working out.

One of the most pleasant and informative ways to see St. Catharines and Port Dalhousie, besides walking their downtown cores and old city centres, is to take advantage of the extensive system of recreation paths created by the Welland Canals Preservation Association.

Each of the four consecutive canals during the Welland Canal's 165-year history is a bit deeper and wider than its predecessor. Only fragments of each remain, however, and the Welland Canals Preservation Association has developed a system of parkland called "The Merritt Trail" that follows the course of the old canals stretching from Lake Erie to Lake Ontario. It is a walking/bicycling/hiking trail connected to a series of interlinking parks set in natural wilderness, interspersed with ruins and structures of historic importance. The Preservation Association has developed a guidebook with maps and annotated explanations of all the sites along the trail, giving you a history of the canal. The sections at Port Dalhousie and St. Catharines are the most complete.

Contact the Welland Canal Preservation Association for a copy of their guidebook, "The Merritt Trail," at P.O. Box 1224, St. Catharines, Ontario, L2R 7A7, (416) 684-1135.

The "sea of masts" at Port Dalhousie in the late 1800s. Note the Port Dalhousie main street in the background.
- St. Catharines Historical Museum

Opposite:
Lighthouse at Port Dalhousie. - Don Mason

The first Welland Canal, now a lovely canal-side garden park.   - Don Mason

Rowers on Henley Island. All rowers are not necessarily big and burly. On the contrary! - Anthony DeAngelo

Opposite: The old carousel at Port Dalhousie. All the animals have been lovingly restored and it's only a nickle a ride!
                                                                    - P. Shipley Fielding

Overleaf: Senior eights at the Henley Regatta.   - Don Mason

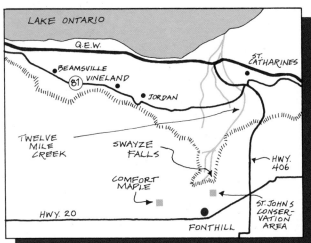

Pelham··
Fonthill

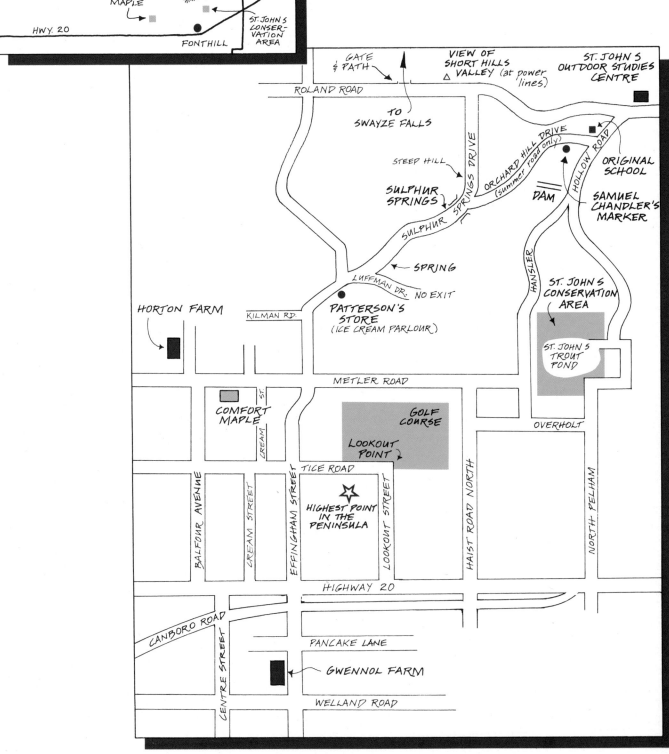

4
Pelham and the Short Hills

On a clear day, you may not be able to see forever, but what you can see is a terrific panoramic view of two Great Lakes, and the skylines of Toronto, Niagara Falls and Buffalo. This most unusual view is seen from the summit of the uplands west of Fonthill, 260 metres (853 feet) above sea level.

Fonthill, in Pelham, is the geographic centre of the region and the highest point of elevation in Niagara. It is the hub from which the entire region below radiates its lush carpet of orchards, vineyards and towns.

So central and so commanding is the view here that during the War of 1812, when the defence of Upper Canada was paramount, it was used as a strategic communications centre. When the officers at Fort George in Niagara (Niagara-on-the-Lake) needed to send word to Fort York (Toronto) to the north or Fort Erie to the south, a signalman, with semaphores and mirrors would mount the hill and flash the message across the lakes.

The war so reaffirmed the military importance of this area that in 1821 the British had 400 acres of land surveyed around the site, including portions of the Short Hills. They proposed to build a ten-sided, star-shaped fortress called "Fort Wellington" as a bulwark "coign of vantage" in the defence of Canada against the United States.

By 1827, however, all plans were abandoned because both available funds and the threat of war had diminished. By 1860 the land was sold to private individuals where it has remained ever since. But it is still possible to get a glimpse of the power of the view from the corner of Tice and Effingham roads or from Lookout Point Golf and Country Club on Lookout Road.

FONTHILL AND THE SHORT HILLS

Both Fonthill and the Short Hills have geological features that differentiate them sharply from the rest of the peninsula. The Short Hills, some of which are preserved as a provincial park, although small in area, are among the most picturesque in southern Ontario. The gently rolling terrain, meandering freshwater streams and steep-sided terraced valleys are punctuated with dozens of sixth-generation "century" farms and the visible remains of early nineteenth-century villages.

Another feature of this area that sets it apart is the existence of preserves of the almost extinct Carolinian forest. (See Introduction)

The area lies in the regional town of Pelham, which includes the hamlets of Pelham Union, North Pelham, Pelham Centre, Ridgeville, Effingham and South Pelham, along with the more urbanized areas of Fonthill and Fenwick. Besides being home to many farming families, it also serves as an affluent bedroom community for many professionals from the surrounding urban centres.

Originally, it too was settled by political and religious refugees and soldiers from the American Revolution who came to farm and rebuild their lives. There are many sixth-generation families still living here whose ancestors faced the uncertain prospects of settlement in the wilderness.

Most farmed, but many provided the services farmers needed. Because of the numerous tributaries of the Twelve Mile Creek, which makes its 22-kilometre (14 miles) trek through Pelham, several successful grist and saw mills lined the streams one after the other.

Pelham had all the potential to develop as a major centre, but from its early history to the present, it was passed by. When St. Catharines was just a settlement, the hamlet of St. John's, near Effingham, was well on its way to becoming a metropolis, but the locating of the Welland Canal in St. Catharines caused it to be passed by.

The British could have had a major fortress here protecting the entire river boundary had they built Fort Wellington, but that too never materialized. At one time Pelham was proposed as the Lincoln County Seat, but Welland County was formed and the City of Welland was chosen instead. Even Laura Secord, on her famous walk to warn the British, took a route just to the north and passed Pelham by. More recently, it was suggested as an ideal location for the site of Brock University but . . .

Overleaf: The Short Hills in Pelham.   - Linda Bramble

What does remain, however, is a pastoral area of gently rolling hills, orchards, vineyards and forests, dotted by old cemeteries, magnificent homes and serene woodlands. Progress forestalled, in this case, has served us well.

The following scenic drive takes you past century-old farms, to spectacular forests, old mills, breathtaking canyons, rolling valleys, pure-water springs, and to the oldest and most venerated sugar maple tree in Canada, the Comfort Maple.

Bring along your walking shoes and a picnic lunch — there are spots which you will find hard to resist.

SCENIC DRIVE

Enter Pelham on Highway 20, either from the west or the east, and turn south on Effingham Road (about 2 kilometres west of Fonthill). The first stop is between Pancake Lane and Welland Road: Gwennol Farm, 1160 Effingham Road, owned and operated by Robin and Barbara Guard. (Gwennol is Cornish for swallow.)

What makes this very old farm very special is the fact that it is a totally organic operation. They use no artificial fertilizers or chemical pesticides in running a mixed farm. They build up the soil, as our ancestors did, using compost and manure, practising companion planting, and rotation of crops with interplantings of herbs and flowers to encourage insects and birds — nature's best pest control.

Their fowl are free range and corn fed, and their sheep are rotated continuously in summer pastures to control parasites. The farm sells fresh produce, dressed fowl, freezer cuts of lamb, tanned lambskins, wool for hand spinning and a wide variety of chemical-free herbs for herb teas, potpourri, herbal baths and seasonings.

From the Gwennol Farm, continue south to Welland Road; turn west and at the next road, Centre, turn right (north) past Canboro, then turn left (west) when you reach Highway 20. Continue briefly on Highway 20 until you reach Balfour Street; turn right (north) and drive until you meet Metler Road. This part of Balfour is like an old country road, with many of its roadside trees standing in spite of the savage and unforgiving blows by hydro road crews.

At Metler Road you can either turn right (east) and head for the Comfort Maple, Canada's largest sugar maple, or take a short side trip to the Horton Farm.

HORTON FARM

To get to the Horton Farm, take a quick jog to the left and then continue with a quick right on Balfour Street. The Horton Farm is just up the road on the left.

The Horton land has been farmed since 1827 by six unbroken generations of Hortons. The large Victorian brick home, typical of many century homes in Pelham, was built in 1870, after the original log home burned. Family history tells of the children being tied to trees to keep them out of danger while the logs were being hewn to make the original home.

Michael Hand, a United Empire Loyalist, received the property from the Crown in 1798. His granddaughter, Abigail Thomas, married another Loyalist, Zephaniah Horton, in 1827, at which time the land was registered in both their names.

The Hortons, originally from England, settled in New Jersey, where Zephaniah was born. Zephaniah later moved to Gainsborough township, then to this farm after his marriage.

Today, Hager Horton and his son Bryant farm the land. In addition to operating it as a dairy farm, they harvest corn, wheat and grapes.

Next stop, the Comfort maple.

THE COMFORT MAPLE

Return along Balfour Street and turn east onto Metler Road. A few metres from the intersection, on the right-hand side, is a small sign (''The Comfort Maple'') by the side of a long drive. At the end of the drive is the 500-year-old ''Old Glory,'' as the Comfort family called her, keeping majestic vigil over the surrounding countryside.

It is estimated that this tree was a sapling when Columbus discovered America, and 100 years old when Champlain set foot in Canada! It reaches a height of 34 metres (112 feet) with a trunk circumference of almost 6 metres (20 feet) just before it divides into two main branches.

The crown forms almost a complete circle extending about 36 metres (118 feet) and spreads 15 to 30 centimetres (6 to 12 inches) a year. Because the tree developed in the open, not crowded by forest, it spread freely. Its leaves are smaller than other maples of its kind, but there are few trees in the world that will fill you with as much awe.

This majestic maple was accepted for preservation by the Niagara Peninsula Conservation Authority from

Opposite: The century farm of the Horton Family, Pelham. - Anthony DeAngelo

The Comfort Maple - 500-year-old "Old Glory" is 34 metres (112 feet) high with a trunk circumference almost 6 metres (20 feet) around. - Anthony DeAngelo

Miss Edna Comfort in memory of her brother Earl Hamden Comfort. The Comfort family still farms the surrounding land, much as their ancestors have since 1816, another testimony to the strong family-farm traditions in Pelham.

Next stop — "Lookout!" — a side trip to catch a glimpse of the view from Fonthill at Lookout Point.

LOOKOUT POINT

Return to Metler Road and proceed east to Effingham Road, turn right (south) to Tice Road. At Tice, turn left (east) and go to the bend of the road at the end. Lookout Golf and Country Club, a private club, occupies the property that provides the best view of the two lakes, but from the entrance to the parking lot corner you can appreciate the scope of the view.

Retrace your steps and return to Effingham Road going north.

If you do not take the side trip, continue on Metler to Effingham and turn north. Just beyond the bend, at the top of the hill, is The Old Ice Cream Parlour, open from spring to fall. Up until the mid-seventies, it carried on a 135-year-old tradition as Effingham's general store

The old Ice Cream Parlour in Pelham, for 135 years a venerable general store. - Anthony DeAngelo

and post office, selling everything from cheese to horse collars. Today it offers a cool & refreshing double dip to the road weary.

ST. JOHN'S CONSERVATION AREA

Just behind the Ice Cream Parlour, on Luffman Road, are the visible remains of some of the many mills that lined the tributaries of the Twelve Mile Creek. Find one where Luffman Road immediately splits into Sulphur Springs Road. Visible to the right is the original wall of a very old mill race (circa 1815).

Further down Sulphur Springs Road, about 47 metres (154 feet) down the bank on the right, is a source of pure spring water percolating through the bedrock. Not many people know about its presence, but those who do return regularly to collect it.

Proceed slowly on Sulphur Springs Road. It is a twisting road with a secondary surface of gravel and sand.

However, the route is worth the inconvenience.

More century farms line this old road. The surrounding woods of all relatively new growth belie the once bustling nature of this entire area. Several mills and mill ponds once lined this route.

Just after a sharp turn, on the left, in the bedrock, near ground level, is a split in the rock. You can locate it by scanning the area for a whitish lining around the rock. Through this split, spring water percolates down, having picked up the sulphur in the layer of gypsum. Voilà! Sulphur Springs.

Next you come to a fork in the road where Orchard Hill intersects Sulphur Springs. Do not take it. The road is treacherous. Stay to the left, go up the rather steep hill, where you meet Roland Road at the top. At this juncture you can either turn right and head for St. John's Conservation area or turn left for a side trip to Short Hills Provincial Park and a hike to Swayze's Falls canyon. (If you choose not to take this hike, save yourself for the walk in St. John's. Swayze's Falls is for the hearty.)

For the side trip to Swayze's Falls, take the second entrance to the park. Park entrances are not easily recognized. Look for the small brown and yellow signs, "Provincial Park Boundary." If you pass a vineyard on the right, you have gone too far. The entrance is just before the vineyard and beside a stand of tall pines. There is a small driveway where you can park your car. To the left of the guardrails that prevent cars from entering the park, there is a narrow footpath. Enter here.

Follow the path straight ahead to the second stream. The first stream has a large culvert and vestiges of an old mill. Continue up the path to first fork; turn right. There are cross-country ski markings on this trail. You will be walking parallel to the second stream all the way to the canyon. If you follow the path through brambles of wild black and red raspberry, thickets of old orchards and rolling woodland, you will discover the falls on your left.

Although a rather tall fence has been constructed for safety, you will be glad it's there, because the chasm is extremely steep. Use extra caution with children.

On the road again and heading for the St. John's Conservation Area, turn right from Sulphur Springs Road onto Roland and drive east.

You will pass some elegant old willows. According to local folklore, the Quakers, who came in the late 1700s, carried their belongings in oxen carts and wagons. When they found the Short Hills, they planted the willow switches they used to prod their oxen, saying, 'We have arrived!' And from these switches the willows grew.

Just before you get to the St. John's Outdoor Centre on the left (it is a different organization from the Conservation Area, so don't be misled), make a country hairpin right-hand turn onto Hollow Road. This road is easy to miss, so do be on the lookout.

At the first road to the right (Orchard Hill Road) is the reconstructed site of the first one-room schoolhouse in the once bustling hamlet of St. John's.

A short side trip down Orchard Hill Drive will take you to the semi-circular grist marker of Samuel Chandler, who was the ringleader in the Short Hills Rebellion of 1837.

Chandler was captured by government troops, sentenced to death, but commuted to life on Van Diemen's Land (Tasmania). He served his sentence for a few years, then made a miraculous escape from the penal colony to the United States. It is reputed that Chandler hid William Lyon Mackenzie for two nights before he too escaped to the U.S.

Return to Hollow Road. Continue down Hollow Road until you reach a 90-degree bend. To the right is the St. John's Conservation Area. If you fish, bring your poles, there is a stocked trout pond inside.

Drive in and park. This is a walk you do not want to miss. The Niagara Peninsula Conservation Authority (Centre Street in Allanburg, near St. Catharines, 227-1013) has compiled a short guide, ''The Sassafras Stroll,'' that will assist you immeasurably in discovering the significance of this area. It is worth obtaining a copy. If you're lucky, there will be copies in a box alongside the trail, but better to obtain a copy ahead of time.

Here is the heart of Niagara's Carolinian forest, the distinctive but diminishing community of plant and animal life found in no other region in Canada.

The one-room school in St. John's on Effingham Rd.   - Don Mason

Opposite:
Dogwood blossoming in the ''Sassafras Stroll'' through the St. John's Conservation Area,
in the heart of the Carolinian forest.   - NPCA

Sassafras blossoms. - Chris Honsberger

The Sassafras Stroll in spring.
- Anthony DeAngelo

St. John's pure-water pond stocked annually with 5,000 rainbow trout.   - NPCA

*Swayze's Falls in the Short Hills
Provincial Park, Pelham.*   - H. Ed Aitken

The St. John's Conservation Area is one of the last remaining public areas left in Ontario to view, first-hand, the over 400 species of plants that grow in the Carolinian zone. Because the area has never been used extensively, rare species have remained intact. Also, there are trees over 200 years old that missed the settlers' axe.

It is a small area, only 78 acres, but the habitat it sustains is rare. Besides sassafras and black walnut, you'll see butternut, shag bark hickory, and wild grape vines spiralling the tallest trees among them, stretching for light.

"It's la-la land in the fall," explains Glenn Meyers of the Niagara Peninsula Conservation Authority. "The birds have a feast feeding on the fermented grapes that grow on the treetops." Particularly significant is the presence of the sparrow-size bluebirds. Once a vanishing breed in this area, their yearly return to St. John's is due not only to the habitat here but to the gentle coaxing of four local naturalists who have provided over 100 nesting sites in holes of trees.

"They used to nest in hollow vineyard fence posts," explains Dr. Ed Aitken, a family physician and one of the naturalists involved. "The fences are solid today to withstand the force of the automatic grape harvesters, so we provided the hollows and these little guys keep coming back every spring."

The walk, groomed with wood chips in low-lying areas, starts beside a bird observation station, where scarlet tanagers, rufous-sided towhees, thrushes, warblers and even mockingbirds can be seen. It then takes you through clear spring-fed ponds, cool and fragrant woodlands, a grove of sassafras trees (the blossoms are extremely fragrant and tea can be made from its bark) and to the trout pond, an angler's heaven. Not only is it a pure-water pond, it is stocked annually with 5,000 to 6,000 rainbow trout. Follow the path to return to your car.

Return to Hollow Road and continue south. Hollow Road becomes North Pelham Road, which takes you back to Highway 20. It is a small region, but so lovely.

The rare mockingbird also
makes its home in Niagara.
- Barry Cherriere

Opposite:
The tiny bluebird, once a vanishing breed in this area, now returns regularly to St. John's.   - H. Ed Aitken

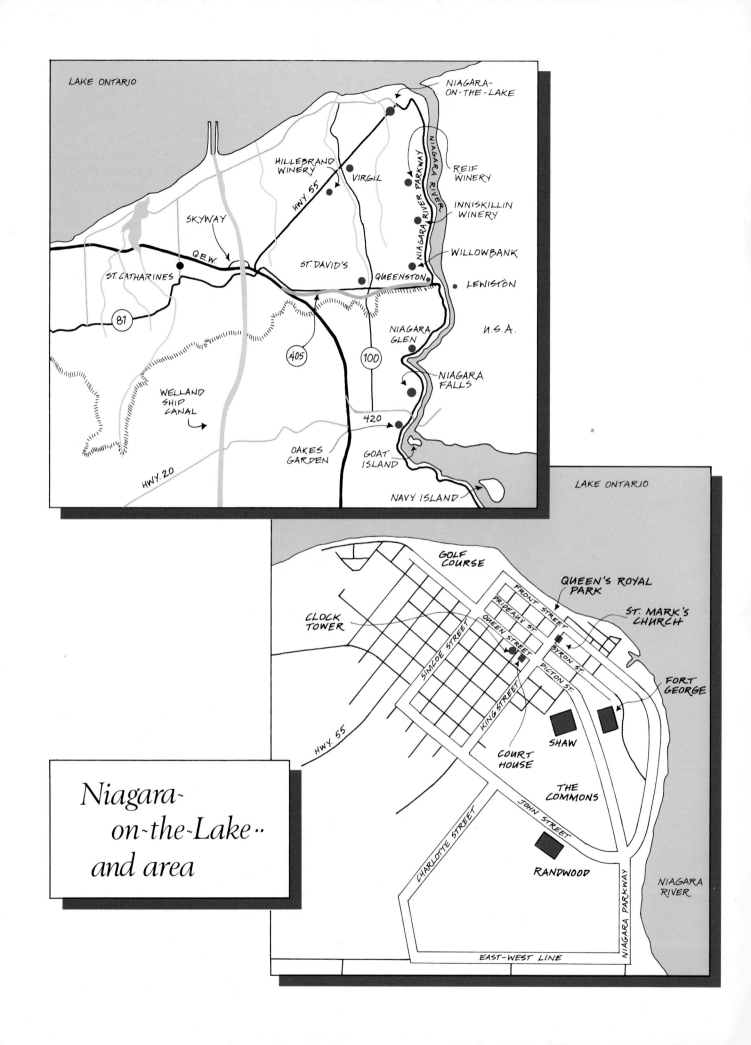

Niagara-
on-the-Lake
and area

5
Niagara-on-the-Lake

Niagara-on-the-Lake, the thriving summer-time retreat for theatregoers and history buffs, keeps the darker secrets of its past to itself. Like a noble family, it stands dignified and resolute. There are no reminders of the days when the town was languishing in apathy and decay.

Its current charm and polish is a relatively recent incarnation. This stately old town has been at different times a legislative, military, shipbuilding, naval and educational centre.

When the Welland Canal came, it decreased the need for Niagara's port access to the lake and, with that, shipbuilding declined and dockyards and factories closed. The town was stricken. Agriculture, commercial fishing and a trickle of tourism kept its heart alive, but it was not until the 1960s that its real renaissance began.

Today, world-class theatre at the Shaw Festival has helped to inject renewed vitality into Niagara-on-the-Lake.

There are many reasons to visit it. Besides the obvious — its summertime cavalcade of plays, exquisite shops, architectural heritage and fine dining — Niagara-on-the-Lake must be celebrated for its distinctive past.

It has been said that to understand the history of Niagara-on-the-Lake is to understand much of the history of early Ontario. It was here that Col. John Butler (the dauntless leader of the famous colonial regiment, Butler's Rangers, who fought for the British during the Revolutionary War) took the first census in Canada (1782), that the first grist mill was built (1783), and where the first legislature in Upper Canada held its sessions (1792).

At the urging of Col. John Graves Simcoe, Upper Canada's first Lieutenant-Governor, the legislature abolished the importation of slaves here in 1793, which gradually made Upper Canada a refuge for thousands of American blacks seeking freedom.

Niagara-on-the-Lake also had the first newspaper, the first agricultural society and the first public library.

In 1813 during the War of 1812, the Americans occupied the town and, before leaving, burned it to the ground. Little remained from the smoking ruins, but still intact was the force of community will which enabled the townspeople to rebuild.

What you see here today are the homes rebuilt after the fire, fortified with strong trees and foundations, classically designed and determined to endure. (The walking tour "Historic Guide: Where Canada Began" is available at any hotel, restaurant or the Chamber of Commerce.)

St. Andrews Church, Niagara-on-the-Lake.
A classic example of Greek Revival built in early
19th century Niagara.   - Don Mason

First it was called simply Niagara, the Anglicized version of an Indian word, Ongniaahra, meaning strait. (Indeed, the Niagara River is not a "river" at all, but rather a strait between two larger bodies of water.) Next it was called Butlersburg, after Col. John Butler, and later West Niagara.

When Governor Simcoe arrived in 1792, he renamed it Newark, after a small town in England. However, tradition and community preference endured and by 1800 the town's name had reverted back to Niagara.

In 1900, in order to help the post office distinguish it from Niagara Falls, the government renamed it the more romantic "Niagara-on-the-Lake."

It began its life absorbing the great influx of Loyalist exiles in 1783. They came from many walks of life — soldiers, wagon drivers, convoys of immigrant farmers, boatmen, spies and drummer boys alike — many travelling hundreds of miles through the wilderness. Most were motivated by loyalty to the crown of England after its devastating defeat by the Americans. Others, such as the "late Loyalists" of the 1790s were understandably attracted by the promise of rich land on easy terms.

Today Niagara-on-the-Lake still attracts thousands of people who come to share its harvest, view the quiet beauty of the lake and river, and for a few brief hours, circle back to meet time.

There are, of course, sites visitors must not miss, such as the Shaw Festival Theatre, Fort George, the Apothecary, the historic churches, the Queen Street shops, the marvellous collection of dearly restored nineteenth-century homes and the Court House. (1847) But if you sneak away, you can also visit places that will give you time to reflect on the lives of the men and women who first charted this province.

QUEEN'S ROYAL PARK

When the sidewalks get too crowded and the food too rich, head for Queen's Royal Park at the mouth of the Niagara River. The best way to get there from Queen Street is to go past the clock tower to King Street and turn left (east) for two blocks. The park is on the left.

With a lunch packed from one of the town's deli's, picnic at this perfect hillside retreat overlooking the American Fort Niagara on the other side. Under century-old trees you can watch billowing multicoloured sails as small fleets of day sailors tack their way through the channel getting ready to face the choppy, colder waters of

Lake Ontario. There is also a small beach below, suitable for sailing toy boats or for simply cooling off walk-weary toes.

ST. MARK'S CEMETERY

Many things about town reveal its history — the museum, the library, the architecture, and the historical plaques. But perhaps the most interesting and usually overlooked places are its cemeteries. The cemetery at St. Mark's Church, the oldest church in town, is no exception. Inscribed on its gravestones is the poetry of another age.

The oldest stone actually dates back ten years before the church was officially declared a parish. It is now mounted on the wall of the north vestibule inside the church. It is a remarkable example of folk art. It reads, "LENERD BLANCK DESEaCED AUGt 5th 1782." "There is pathos in this humble effort," writes former minister Rev. Hugh Maclean, "which makes the observer long to be able to know about the personalities involved and also to be able to assure the unknown recorder that his record has survived for 200 years."

When the town was captured by American armies in May of 1813, they used the church as a hospital and storehouse. To the southeast of the church there is still a trench that leads to the river. There is also evidence they used the gravestones for practical and rather irreverent purposes. One very flat stone was used by army butchers as a chopping block. Although its surface is marred by deep scores, its inscription is a defiant and ironic survival of both time and the butcher's cleaver. It is the gravestone of Charles Morrison, a valiant magistrate and merchant who was a "loyalist to his Sovereign."

There are many consoling inscriptions, such as the one for little Ann Graham, who died March 2, 1892, age 4 years:

> "My time is short; the longer my rest
> God called me heare because he
> thought it best
> So weep not; drie up your tears
> Heare must i lie till Christ apears."

Other inscriptions are more profound queries into the meaning of life, such as the inscription for June Cassady, who died on May 27, 1813:

> "Man's life what is it? Tis a flower
> Looks fresh and dies within the hour."

Queen's Royal Park, Niagara-on-the-Lake.   - Anthony DeAngelo

Where Niagara's waters meet Lake Ontario's — the view from Queen's Royal Park.   - Don Mason

Overleaf:
Sailboats crossing the channel in front of the American Fort Niagara across the bay.   - Don Mason

Randwood, one of Niagara's architectural delights.   - Anthony DeAngelo

St. Mark's Church and cemetery.   - Ben Bramble

Clock tower, Niagara-on-the-Lake.   - Don Mason

If you head south from St. Mark's Church you will eventually reach the romantic Niagara River Parkway. Take this route, which parallels the wine route, to visit three of Ontario's most popular wineries — Willowbank, Reif and Inniskillen. Each provides tasting opportunities to sample their prize-winning wines.

As Niagara-on-the-Lake is more than just a theatre town, it is also more than just the tiny village by the lake. In January 1970 the Township of Niagara and the village were amalgamated into the Regional Town of Niagara-on-the-Lake as were many hamlets and villages across the Peninsula. Consequently, when you speak of Niagara-on-the-Lake today you must also include the vineyards and orchards that are bounded by Lake Ontario, the Niagara River, the escarpment, and the land adjoining the Welland Canal. This area includes the little hamlets of St. Davids, Virgil and Queenston.

QUEENSTON

Like Niagara-on-the-Lake, Queenston began in the last years of the eighteenth century. When Gov. Simcoe arrived, the town, originally known as West Landing, became the location of the barracks for the governor's new regiment, the Queen's Rangers. Soon the settlement's name progressed from Queen's Town to Queenston.

Its location was ideal for development, located just a few miles downstream from the Falls and at the end of navigation from Lake Ontario, where entrepreneurs developed a busy portage route to Chippewa for goods passing from Lake Ontario to Lake Erie.

The Battle of Queenston Heights, during the War of 1812, cost the life of the esteemed general, Sir Isaac Brock, commander of the British regulars and Canadian militia. A 61-metre (200 feet) monument in Queenston Park commemorates his distinction and valour.

Lovely walks abound in this pleasing town though it sports none of Niagara-on-the-Lake's sophistication. Starting at Brock's monument in Queenston Park, you can walk down the steps and out through the wrought-iron gates of the park to a spectacular *belle vue* overlooking the river gorge and the village of Queenston. Across the river is Queenston's American counterpart, Lewiston, New York, home of the splendid Artpark Theatre. The panorama shows a wider, more subdued river as it winds through orchards and vineyards to enter Lake Ontario at Niagara-on-the-Lake.

In the autumn, bird-watchers come to this area by the thousands to get a glimpse of the gulls from the docks at Queenston. Naturalists claim it is the best place in the world to see up to 13 species of gulls and many ducks

Ring-bill colony, Queenston   - H. Ed Aitken

Opposite: Brock's Monument, Queenston.   - Ben Bramble

Overleaf: Belle vue of Niagara River from Queenston Heights.   - Ben Bramble

who visit the river during their migration south. Species such as Bonaparte's gull and the herring gull are plentiful, but the rarer European "little gulls," black-headed Sabene's gull, glaucous and Ireland gulls may also be sighted.

The Queenston docks can be reached by taking any of the streets off Queenston Street, and then heading down to the river. If you take Queenston Street to Dumfries and continue down Dumfries to the river, you will find a sandy road at the end that winds its way to the river's edge. Lewiston, New York, and Artpark can be seen directly across the river.

NIAGARA FALLS

Niagara Falls has few secrets left. Still, it does offer to its millions of annual guests its most cherished secret, but few ever bother to learn of it. Usually, visitors walk to the precipice, feel the spray lace their faces, listen to the thunder of the upper lakes waters as they plunge down, and think secretly, "Is that all there is?" Then they visit some attractions, trek through the commercial districts of town, buy a few mementos and drive away, their memory of nature's magnificence diminished by the gilt of commerce.

It need not be so. There are ways to appreciate this wonder of the world without being sidetracked. Learning the secrets of Niagara Falls requires either the stamina to participate in its majesty or the serenity to view it quietly, preferably both.

The Falls originated when the Niagara Escarpment was the shoreline of an inland sea, Lake Iroquois, that covered much of North America. The soil and rock that comprise the escarpment are variegated sandwiches of hard and soft materials. As the waters of the Niagara River flowed over its crest, they washed away and undercut the lower layers of softer rock. As the overhanging upper layers grew increasingly unstable from lack of supporting rock below, they fell off and the Falls receded, moving upstream at a steady rate. Geologists estimate that about 14,000 years ago the present site of the Falls was 6 kilometres (4 miles) downstream. Up until 1900 it had receded at the astonishing rate of about 1 metre (3.3 feet) a year. Since then, through control features and diversionary measures, recession has been slowed significantly.

OAKES GARDEN THEATRE

Adjacent to Queen Victoria Park is the best panoramic view of the Falls — the beautiful amphitheatre and floral gardens of Oakes Garden Theatre. It is located on the site of the once world-famous Clifton Hotel, which burned in 1932. Sir Harry Oakes, the millionaire prospector and mining engineer (later murdered mysteriously in Bermuda), purchased the property then presented it to the Niagara Parks Commission in exchange for property on the hill overlooking Victoria Park — hardly an equitable exchange.

The fan-shaped amphitheatre suggests the theatres of ancient Greece. A curved pergola connects two other pavilions, one oriented to view the Horseshoe Falls and the other to view the American Falls.

The formal gardens and sloping terraces are unexcelled. It is an often-missed oasis of peace amidst the crush of tourists who clamour for space near the Falls.

THE GLEN

A little known horticulture feature to be found in the Niagara Parks Commission gardens is their newly established fragrance garden, located north of the present Niagara Parks Greenhouse. Both indoor and outdoor gardens are open to the public free of charge. The garden is at its best in summer and particularly popular with the visually handicapped. It has over 100 different species of plants known for their texture and aroma, including sage, thyme, rosemary, heliotrope, linden and rose. It is signed for the visually handicapped.

But it is The Glen that invites you to share the primeval secrets of the Falls themselves. The parking lot to The Glen is located on the Niagara River Parkway just 3 kilometres (2 miles) below the Falls. The Glen is accessible only by descending a winding precipitous path from the cliffs above. Each step you take down the flight of stone steps to the river's edge below brings you 8,000 years closer to the genesis of the river's ancient bed.

There are jumbles of boulders, narrow passageways, forest-cool paths, potholes, teetering rocks and over 50 species of wildflowers on its 4 kilometres (2.5 miles) of paths. It is second only to the Falls in natural Carolinian beauty.

Our tour of Undiscovered Niagara ends ironically at one of the most discovered places in the world. All the more reason to see it again, from a different point of view, and perhaps, as T.S. Elliot suggested, to begin to know it for the first time. Like this river boundary, our imaginations tend to construct boundaries, but if gently and joyfully nudged, they too can be crossed.

Oakes Garden, Niagara Falls, an oasis of peace. - Anthony DeAngelo

Overleaf: Niagara Falls. - Niagara Parks Commission

Oakes Hall, once the home of Sir Harry Oakes, now the offices of the Niagara Parks Commission.

- Linda Bramble

Old Toronto Power Station, Niagara Falls. - Linda Bramble

Opposite: The Gorge. - Niagara Parks Commission

Bibliography

Carnochan, Janet. *History of Niagara.* Mika Publishing, Belleville, Ontario, 1973.

Collins, Brian. *"Discovery of Indian Houses Hailed as a Significant Find."* St. Catharines Standard, June 28, 1980.

Cooper, S.J. Howard and Sewell T. *Try Walking Your Niagara,* St. Catharines, 1983.

Fields, John. *Bicentennial Stories of Niagara-on-the-Lake.* Rannie, Lincoln, Ontario, 1981.

Fitzpatrick, Peter, ed. *Merritt Trail Guide: An Historic Journey through Port Dalhousie, St. Catharines and Merritton.* Welland Canals Preservation Association, St. Catharines, Ontario, 1985.

Gillard, William and Tooke, Thomas. *The Niagara Escarpment From Tobermory to Niagara Falls,* U of T Press, Toronto, 1975.

Grimsby Historical Society, *Once Upon a Little Town: Grimsby 1876-1976.* Grimsby Historical Society, 1979.

Jadeson, John and Addis, Fred A. *The Welland Canals: A Comprehensive Guide,* Welland Canals Foundation, St. Catharines, 1982.

Kenyon, Walter A. *Geometry of Death: The Neutral Indian Cemetery at Grimsby.* Monograph. Available at Grimsby Museum.

Lincoln County 1856-1956. Lincoln County Council, St. Catharines, 1956.

Maclean, Rev. Hugh D. *A Rare Gift Within Its Gates: The Story of St. Mark's Anglican Church, Niagara-on-the-Lake,* T & C Associates, 1980.

Meyers, Glenn A. *The Niagara Escarpment: Why it is, What it is.* Manuscript, 1966.

Niagara Conservation Authority, *"The Sassafras Stroll"* (pamphlet) The St. John's Conservation Area.

Ontario Editorial Bureau. *Byways of Lincoln County.* Monograph. St. Catharines, 1968.

Ontario Geneological Society (Niagara Branch). *Notes From Niagara: A Walking Tour of Jordan.* St. Catharines, Ontario.

Pelham Historical Society. *Pelham Historical Calendar (1977).*

Rannie, William F. *Cave Springs Farm in Lore and Legend,* W.F. Rannie, Beamsville, Ontario, 1981.

Shipley, Robert. *St. Catharines: Garden on the Canal.* Windsor Publications, Burlington, Ontario, 1987.

Stokes, Peter John. *Old Niagara-on-the-Lake,* U of T Press, Toronto, 1971.

Taylor, Robert. *Discovering St. Catharines Heritage: The Old Town,* LACAC, St. Catharines, 1981.

Tovell, Walter M. *The Niagara Escarpment.* ROM, U of T Press, Toronto, 1966.

Turcotte, Dorothy. *Greetings From Grimsby Park: The Chautauqua of Canada.* Grimsby Historical Society, 1985.

Index

Balls Falls 8, 9
Beamer Point 21, 22
Beamsville 21
Brock's Monument (Queenston) 73
Canterbury Cottage (Grimsby) 15, 16
Carolinian forest 9, 51, 58-63, 76
Cave Spring Farm (Beamsville) 20, 21
Chestnut Hall (Vineland) 27
Clock Tower (Niagara-on-the-Lake) 71
Comfort Maple (Pelham) 54, 56
DeCew Falls and Morningside Mill (St. Catharines) 43
Farewell House (Grimsby) 17
Fonthill (Pelham) 51
Fragrance Garden (Niagara Parks, Niagara Falls) 76
Fry House (Jordan) 27, 28
Gibson House (Grimsby) 16
Glen, the (Niagara Falls) 76
Grimsby 12-23
Gwennol Farm (Pelham) 54
Hawks at Beamer Point (Grimsby) 20
Henley Island (St. Catharines) 45, 47-49
Horticultural Research Institute (Vineland) 32
Horton Farm (Pelham) 53, 54
Ice cream parlour, the old (Pelham) 57
Indian dig (Grimsby) 18
Jordan and Vineland 24-35
Lookout Point (Pelham) 57
Maps: Grimsby 12; Jordan and Vineland 24;
      Niagara-on-the-Lake and Niagara Falls 64;
      Pelham and the Short Hills 50;
      St. Catharines 36
Marketsquare (St. Catharines) 42
Merritt, William Hamilton (St. Catharines) 37
Methodist Campground Temple (Grimsby) 13
Montebello Park (St. Catharines) 41
Morningstar Mill and DeCew Falls (St. Catharines) 5
Nelles Manor (Grimsby) 15

Neutral Indians, discovery of (Grimsby) 17, 18
Niagara Falls 76, 77
Niagara Escarpment at Beamer Point (Grimsby) 21
Niagara Peninsula Conservation Authority
Niagara River (view from Queenston) 74
Niagara River Parkway recretion trail (opposite) 10
Niagara Wine Region (information) 10
Oakes Garden Theatre (Niagara Falls) 76, 77
Oakes Hall (Niagara Falls) 80
Pelham and the Short Hills 50-63
Port Dalhousie (St. Catharines) 45
Port Dalhousie light houses (St. Catharines) 44, 45
Queen's Royal Park (Niagara-on-the-Lake) 66, 67
Queenston 72
Queenston docks 76
Randwood (Niagara-on-the-Lake) 70
Rockway (Jordan)
    cemetery 30, 31
    gorge 35
    falls 1
St. Andrews Church (Grimsby) 14
St. Andrews Church (Niagara-on-the-Lake) 65
St. John's Conservation Area 57
St. John's one room school house 58
St. Mark's Cemetery (Niagara-on-the-Lake) 66, 70
St. Catharines 36-49
Sassafras Stroll, the 58-60
Short Hills 50-53
Sugarbush at Vineland Quarries 29
Swayze's Falls 57, 61
Toronto Power Station, the old 80
Upper Falls in Jordan (opposite) 35
Vineland (and Jordan) 24-35
Vineland Estate Vineyards 31
Welland Canal 37-39
Welland Canal, the old 41, 47
Welland Hotel (nineteenth century photo) 40

ABOUT THE AUTHOR

LINDA BRAMBLE is a freelance writer living in St. Catharines with her husband Ben. She has taught university (philosophy and psychology), has been an educational consultant, and has spoken frequently on local history. *Undiscovered Niagara* afforded her the wonderful opportunity to combine her love of history and travel with her pride and love for Niagara. Her next book traces U.S./Confederate espionage along the border in mid-nineteenth century Niagara.

ABOUT THE PHOTOGRAPHERS

DR. ED AITKEN, when not photographing nature through his hobby as a naturalist, practices family medicine in Grimsby, Ontario and is a professor at McMaster's School of Medicine.

ANTHONY DEANGELO, a graduate of Pittsburgh Institute of Art, is a prize-winning commercial photographer living and working in Ohio.

DR. DON MASON is a pathologist with St. Catharines General Hospital and in his spare time has also, for many years, chronicled photographically the life and times of the Niagara region.

ALSO: Veronica Reiser, Chris Honsberger, Barry Cherriere, D. Free, David Street, Linda and Ben Bramble, P. Shipley Fielding.